Why you should read *Coaching in Ministry*

"If you've heard about how coaching can help and are ready to wade in, but don't want to commit to a big program, *Coaching in Ministry* is what you've been looking for. Taste and see."

— **Dr. Bob Logan**
Church Consultant & Coach,
loganleadership.com

"Through careful inquiry, people can be taught without being told. This kind of servanthood needs to be recovered by the church if we are to equip normal people to make disciples who make disciples."

— **Jeff Vanderstelt**
Soma visionary leader, pastor at Doxa Church,
Author of *Saturate*

"How do we as ministry leaders really inspire people to a lifetime of discipleship? *Coaching in Ministry* points us to a mindset and a skill set that … introduces ministry leaders to a profound way of 'exponentially multiplying leadership development'."

— **Jane Creswell**
ICF Master Certified Coach,
Author, *Christ-Centered Coaching*

"Keith's book *The COACH Model for Christian Leaders* is a must read and now we can add *Coaching in Ministry* to that list!"

— **Larry Barker**
Director of Church Planting for BMA Missions

GW00537523

"I have not found a discipline as effective and empowering as coaching to help people keep in step with the Holy Spirit. *Coaching in Ministry* is a timely introduction to the potential and power of coaching."

—Eddie Hancock
Lead Pastor, First Southern Baptist Church,
Caldwell, Idaho

"I have personally benefitted from [Keith's] insights, and I have sent many of my teammates through his excellent coaching program. *Coaching in Ministry* is concise, grounded, and practical."

—Ken Cochrum
VP of Global Digital Strategies at Cru
Author of *CLOSE*

"Great coaches help you get to where you need to go, and they help you become the person God intends. Master these principles and practices and the fruit will be transformed lives and ministries."

—Steve Addison
Author of *What Jesus Started*

"A skill that's desperately needed for those in engaged in ministry — regardless of the culture or the context — is coaching. And there is no one in the world whom I trust better to deliver and train such skills than Keith Webb."

— Dr. Sam Metcalf
President, Church Resource Ministries-US

"Jesus didn't merely recruit people – He developed them! Keith Webb provides a practitioners guide to developing leaders. He does a nice job clarifying how coaching is different (not better) from other important ministry methods."

— Dino Senesi
Church Planter Coaching Leader

"If there was one skill that every leader would benefit from by adding to their portfolio, it would be coaching. This book is a wonderful primer for how coaching can make a significant impact on bringing out the best in those you lead."

— Dr. Dennis W Easter
Supervisor, SoCAL Foursquare Churches

"*Coaching In Ministry* is an excellent tool and an easy read. Keith is a master at equipping people to coach well and his book, *Coaching in Ministry,* oozes with his expertise."

— Gary Mayes, D.Min.
Executive Director of ChurchNEXT at CRM,
Author of *DNA of a Revolution*

"I am excited about *Coaching In Ministry* as Keith shows ministry leaders how to truly multiply leaders in a ministry context."

— Brian Howard
Executive Director, Context Coaching, Inc.

"If you're in ministry and have wondered what coaching is all about, whether it's for you, or how to implement it, Keith Webb's, *Coaching In Ministry* needs to be the next book you read."

— Michael John Cusick
Author of *Surfing for God*,
President, Restoring the Soul

"As a missionary and a pastor who has experienced the power of coaching, I highly recommend this book to everyone who wants to actively help others become more effective and successful in Kingdom work."

— Brian Ingraham
Sr. Pastor, Re:Hope Next Generation Bible
Church, Glasgow, Scotland

"With straight-forward focus, *Coaching in Ministry*, gets to the heart of the what and why of ministry coaching. Dr. Keith Webb has concisely provided an overview of the potential of coaching as a tool for life change."

— Rev. Charles N. Hooper, Jr.
Director, Life on Life Ministries,
Perimeter Church in Atlanta, Georgia

"Keith Webb has trained hundreds of pastors, missionaries and ministry leaders to embrace a coaching posture. In *Coaching in Ministry* he provides the basic understanding and tools you need to increase your effectiveness today."

— Dave DeVries
Coach, Trainer, Strategist with
Missional Challenge

"Some books are written from knowledge and research, others are written from an author's passion, calling and experience. Keith writes from all of these. Each page exudes Keith's passion to see leaders thrive in ministry and multiply their influence."

— Bryan Brown
Director, International Leadership Development,
Perimeter Church in Atlanta, Georgia

"Our friend Keith Webb in his new book *Coaching in Ministry* has done a masterful job to help all of us increase our leadership development effectiveness 10X by following Jesus' coaching model."

— Bob Tiede
Leadership Development Team at Cru,
Blogger at LeadingWithQuestions.com

"Keith Webb has provided the coach training that is revolutionising the way we multiply Fresh Expressions of Church in the UK. If you're looking for a brief introduction to the subject, *Coaching in Ministry* provides a brilliant apologetic for Christian coaching."

— Graham Horsley
Missioner for Fresh Expressions UK

"...*Coaching in Ministry* will sharpen both your thinking and skills as you lead others to expand the kingdom of God."

— Bryan Wintersteen
Global Missions Pastor,
Briarwood Presbyterian Church

COACHING IN MINISTRY

HOW BUSY CHURCH LEADERS CAN MULTIPLY THEIR MINISTRY IMPACT

ALSO BY KEITH E. WEBB

The COACH Model for Christian Leaders

Coaching in Asia: The First Decade
(with Denise Wright, Anna Leong, and Sam Chia, eds.)

Overcoming Spiritual Barriers in Japan

Sherlock Holmes in Japan

Coaching In Ministry

How Busy Church Leaders Can Multiply Their Ministry Impact

Keith E. Webb

Active Results LLC

Coaching In Ministry: How Busy Church Leaders Can
Multiply Their Ministry Impact

Active Results LLC
www.activeresults.com

ISBN 10: 0-9665658-2-7
ISBN 13: 978-0-9665658-2-9

First Printing: June 2015

Scripture taken from the HOLY BIBLE, NEW INTER-
NATIONAL VERSION®. Copyright © 1973, 1978,
1984 by International Bible Society. Used by permis-
sion of Zondervan. All rights reserved.

To Dr. Steve Ogne

Table of Contents

Discover How Coaching Can Multiply Your Ministry Impact

"I haven't told this to anyone, but I'm thinking of leaving the ministry," confided Terry, a pastor of a church in Seattle.

Terry and I met at a conference. When he found out I coached Christian leaders and had ministry experience he shared his difficulties with me. He explained that for the past three years he had felt isolated and experienced frequent interpersonal conflict with a board member. Ministry results were slow. Worse, he was worn out. He felt like he and his wife were in charge of everything at his church.

Terry had tried to get people "to serve" and "get involved" in ministries. People were busy and unresponsive, so he kept running most of the ministries himself or leaving them undone. He had run out of ideas. His vision for ministry had slowly drained from him. And now he was ready to quit.

Terry needed more than an encouraging pat on the back or a couple hours of listening and advice. He needed a different approach to ministry. And he needed someone who would walk with him through these challenges.

Terry's case is not unusual; in fact, it is all too common. Perhaps you can relate to Terry. You want to see people engaged in ministry, and growing as leaders. You want to know what it takes to make a greater impact.

Shortly after our initial conversation, Terry attended *The Coaching Workshop for Christian Leaders*. We got together a few months later. As he began talking I could see Terry was a changed man, much more vibrant, with a smile on his face.

Terry told me what had happened over the previous few months. "Many of my habits as a leader were challenged," Terry said. "I realized that I like being the 'answer-man' and the center of things. Yet, my work as a pastor is to help people hear from God, and not just through my teaching. I decided to try an experiment. I started asking more questions and listening. Listening not in order to give a response, but listening to hear what the person was saying, not saying, and what God may be saying to him."

Terry saw people grow and change. "I shifted my approach to discipleship and leadership development to more of a dialogue. I'm still teaching, but now I use a question-listening approach when I meet with people so they can make better personal applications."

Terry also realized how tightly he held onto ministry efforts at the church. He wanted things done a certain way and if people didn't do them that way, he did it himself. As he listened to other people's ideas and approaches and explored them by asking questions. "I'm seeing people come up with next steps for ministries that never occurred to me. The best part is: since it's their idea, they own it!"

One of the biggest results for Terry was an emotional one. "I've been overwhelmed to the point of exhaustion trying to figure out how to move people into real discipleship. That burden has been lifted from my shoulders. I don't have to have the all answers or keep things running. God is at work. As people engage with what God is doing in their lives, they grow, change, and engage in ministry naturally. I've still got plenty of pressures, but at the same time I feel a freedom I haven't feel in a long time."

Confessions from a Ministry Leader

Allow me to share some of my story. Over the past 25 years, I've been involved in many different ministry initiatives including church planting in Japan, leadership development in Indonesia, and building a global coaching training ministry.

It hasn't been easy, and to be honest, until lately, not as fruitful as I hoped.

You see, until a few years ago, I had a ton of vision, but not the skills needed to develop other people around me while doing the ministry.

Are You Reaching Your Ministry Potential Or Ready to Quit?

Personally, I know how challenging it can be to minister. Whether you are pastoring a church or ministering in a foreign country or supervising small group leaders, it's tough.

Perhaps you can relate to these statistics:

- 57% of pastors say they would quit if they had another job[1].

- 5.5% of cross-cultural ministers leave the field each year, most of them for preventable reasons[2].

Most of these are experienced ministers, not people in their first years of ministry. They are weary. Years of carrying the burden of keeping things going weighs on them.

I know what it feels like to be spread thin, like butter scraped over too much bread. And the pace is only speeding up. People are more spread out. The demands on our time are increasing. It's hard to keep up!

Ministry is not getting simpler, it is becoming more complex.

I thought if I could just work smarter, more efficiently, I could see the ministry impact I hoped for. However, it wasn't enough. There were just too many needs and too much to do.

Churches are growing – if not in membership, at least in activity! Consider how much goes into running a church these days. A worship team, children's ministry, student ministries, community groups, local and global outreach, and in many cases, a multimedia production team – are all par for the course. The list of "moving parts" seems endless and ever-growing.

While all these activities can lead to a healthy church, each of them require an asset so vital, so rare, and so costly to obtain that many churches are outgrowing their ability to produce them. What asset am I referring to?

Godly leaders.

For many ministry leaders, particularly pastors, training and developing leaders for ministry is one of their most significant challenges.

Imagine trying to run a Sunday school ministry without leaders. Imagine facilitating small groups throughout your city without leaders. Impossible! Oh, the problems we could solve if we had a steady supply of leaders!

But this, as we both know, is not the case. And that's the rub. As much as pastors and ministers have been trained to teach the Word of God, we have been left to fend for ourselves when it comes to meeting the demands of the modern day church and all its moving parts.

I tried to get around it. "Recruit other leaders to join you," was the advice I received. I did. The administrative load multiplied with each new teammate. *Soon I was busy filling out forms instead of building into the lives of others.*

Simply bringing on a new hire to offset my to-do list did not solve the roadblocks I was running into. I don't tell you this to discourage you. Rather, I want to be real about the challenges we face.

Developing myself and others to be effective in ministry turned out to be my biggest challenge of all. Like Pastor Terry's story at the beginning of this chapter, the solution required a complete shift in how I developed leaders, my organization, and ultimately myself.

I realized: If I didn't approach ministry in new ways, then my ministry would likely never reach its potential. I didn't want that and I don't want that for you.

I found an extremely practical solution to multiply ministry AND develop others — even those who live at a distance from you.

It's called coaching.

Everyone means something different when they use the word "coach." So, let me share what I mean by that.

I began coaching when I lived in Indonesia as a way to help emerging Indonesian leaders find their own answers rather than just listening to mine. I wanted them to hear from God (not just me), discern together as a group His direction, and follow it. I found I was unequipped to do that. I knew how to teach and preach. I knew how to advise and counsel. But I didn't know how to help people without giving my ideas, solutions, and input.

I found a solution with coaching – listening and asking powerful questions to draw out from leaders what God had put in.

Coaching transformed the way I do ministry, and more importantly, it transformed my view of how God grows leaders, including me.

I ended up writing my Doctor of Ministry project about how to develop indigenous Indonesian leadership through coaching. My learning turned into an interactive workshop and the book, *The COACH Model For Christian Leaders*, so others could learn how to integrate coaching skills into their leadership style.

This is not to point to my personal accomplishments, but rather the transformation I experienced as a result of implementing coaching skills into my ministry. I never imagined I could have that kind of impact before I learned how to coach.

I believe, deep down inside, you are looking for an answer to a very specific problem: that of developing leaders inside a volunteer organization with a limited budget.

The challenges of vocational ministry, particularly for pastors, are unique. This is not like business, where the motivations of workers often center on their paycheck or position. You need a unique approach, methodology, and solution.

In this book, I'll show you it's possible to multiply your ministry and to develop others around you.

You can:

- Reach ministry goals and develop other people along the way.

- Replace your burden of having all the answers with the freedom of having the right questions.

- Stop lamenting over the lack of new leaders and develop the ones you have.

- Overcome the awkwardness of supervising people who are also your friends.

- Multiply your ministry impact.

This book will challenge some of the assumptions you may have about developing leaders. My goal is to do more than challenge, I want to serve you by showing you it is possible to develop leaders and have more impact — while also having more margin in your life. These things are not mutually exclusive.

The world needs your leadership. I do not say this lightly. Each of us carries a unique call from God integral to His plan. Yet, there are no guarantees each of us will complete all that we're able to do. I believe that you are actively seeking new ways to grow yourself and the people you lead. Coaching is a key to multiplying your ministry impact in a healthy way.

1.
What "Coach" Really Means, And Why It Matters

Coaching and athletics are strongly linked in our minds. When I tell people I train leaders in coaching skills, they often ask, "Oh? For what sport?"

Ask anyone what a coach does, and they will likely refer to sports. Regardless of our personal feelings toward those coaching our favorite sports teams, most people think a coach's job is to instruct, yell, and discipline players in an effort to win at all costs.

This was not always the case! In fact, the roots of coaching trace back in history to a village in Hungary and have very little to do with athletics.

The history of the word "coach" is instructive. Here is the story.

It all began in the Little Hungarian Plains of northwest Hungary in the village of Kocs. In the late 15th century, the village of Kocs made its living from building carts and transporting goods. Around 1494, the people of Kocs created a cart with several unique features.

Hungarian King Mátyás was impressed and adopted this cart for the mail route between Vienna and Budapest. News of the wagon of Kocs – the *kocsi* – spread quickly around Europe and became the must-have vehicle of royalty and the rich.

Over the next century the *kocsi* exploded in popularity. This new wagon was subsequently copied throughout Europe. The term *kocsi* became *kutsche* in German, *coche* in French, and *coach* in English. The legacy of the wagons of Kocs is undeniable. It was the starting point of what we know as stagecoaches, motor coaches, and air coaches. It's also the origin of sports coaches, life coaches, and executive coaches.

Coach as a Metaphor

Our modern-day use of the word "coach" is actually a metaphor. As the coach wagon was a means to carry goods from one place to another, the term "coach" evolved and began to be applied to education. In 18th century England, tutors prepped students to pass their exams. The slang reference for tutors became "coach" because tutors quickly and comfortably carried students to their goal of passing their exams.

It wasn't until the late 1880s when the term coach was applied to athletic coaches. They were called "coachers." The image of sports coaching became more of an army drill sergeant than a comfortable carriage or even a tutor.

This association is unfortunate. Let's get that image out of our minds so we can tap into the extraordinary power of coaching in leadership.

What A Coach Does

I define coaching as: an ongoing intentional conversation that empowers a person or group to fully live out God's calling[3].

Coaching focuses on people's learning rather than us teaching. Coachees (those who are coached) are in the driver's seat. They choose their own growth goals, reflect deeply on their current situation, think through their options, and decide their next steps. All the while, the coach actively listens and asks reflective questions, supportively challenging limited beliefs and behaviors.

In practice,

- **A coach focuses on the agenda of the coachee.** The coachee decides which goals or problems to work on, not the coach.

- **A coach uses powerful questions to generate new learning.** The coach does not teach or advise, but rather asks questions and listens.

- **A coach encourages action.** The coachee develops his or her own action steps, not the coach.

- **A coach supports change.** A coach follows-up to support personal learning, growth, and change, rather than demanding change.

The practice of coaching in leadership development is actually a throwback to the historic roots of the Kocs wagon. A coach figuratively "carries" a person to his or her desired destination through ongoing conversations, thought-provoking questions, and support.

Coaching may sound great, but you may be wondering how this fits with teaching. After all, didn't Jesus *tell* people what to do and how to believe? Aren't the Ten Commandments rather clear in *telling* us what God's expectations are of us in terms of lifestyle? Developing leaders requires that we *teach* and *train* others, does it not?

Yes, yes, and yes!

You'll get no argument from me. I love to teach and do regularly. The question is: What teaching methods are most effective for developing leaders? There's more to teaching than telling. It been shown again and again that adults learn better through dialogue and discovery than by someone lecturing to them.

Think of how you like to learn. Maybe you can relate to Winston Churchill when he said, "I am always ready to learn although I do not always like being taught."

As we develop leaders, I want to suggest a different approach - integrating coaching skills. Leaders are developed through a mysterious mixture of reflection, experience, ideation, authenticity, critical thinking, and guidance. It can be a messy process. Coaching, and the framework I will show you, helps shape this process.

Coaching Develops People Holistically

You are busy, and so are your leaders. A coaching style allows you to develop both skills and character. It gets to deeper issues of calling and identity too. Let me share some of my experience.

For 20 years I lived in Japan, Indonesia, and Singapore and worked with Church Resource Ministries, a non-profit organization focused on leadership development. I found a large part of my Western leadership processes did not work in these settings. I needed a more universal approach, something that applied to human beings regardless of race, gender, or cultural contexts. This challenge led me to dig deeper into what the core needs of all human beings are, and better methods of how to develop leaders.

We know the basic human needs are food, clothing, and shelter. But what about our basic emotional needs? The list is widely debated but for simplicity's sake let's assume we all have a need for significance, identity, and love.

The way to exponentially multiply leadership development is to tap into the very needs God created us to have, and utilize an approach that meets those intrinsic needs.

God uniquely created each person to *become* someone special and to *do* something special. This is *calling*. Calling is not just for certain people. Every believer has a calling in at least three areas of his or her life: calling to character or personal holiness (Eph. 1:4), calling to relationship with God (Eph. 1:5), and calling to ministry — a unique contribution to God's kingdom (Eph. 2:10).

Since the practice of coaching is a personalized approach, the process honors the uniqueness of people and God's calling in their lives by not simply assigning them tasks we need done.

A coaching approach creates a supportive environment to help a person "discover" what God has for him or her. People can often find their own answers but may need help getting there. This process prepares them to find their own answers when the coach is not around. And that's leadership development.

We've just scratched the surface. Let's move to the next chapter and talk about one of the most common questions I am asked when it comes to coaching: "Aren't coaching and mentoring the same thing?"

2.
Aren't Coaching and Mentoring the Same Thing?

As a professional coach, I am frequently asked what the difference is between mentors and coaches. Many people assume the two words mean the same thing. While there are significant differences between mentoring and coaching, the bottom line is we need both.

By and large, most ministry leaders are familiar with mentoring. We understand the value of developing leaders, and the personal fulfillment that comes from taking someone "under our wing" to help that person grow, mature, and thrive. The process becomes even more rewarding when that person helps shoulder the load of our ministry.

Mentors Put In

If we were to describe mentoring in a nut-shell, most of us would agree mentoring involves impartation — we are "putting in" insight, strategy, or methodology into another person.

Authors Paul Stanley & J. Robert Clinton define mentoring this way: "Mentoring is a relational process in which a mentor, who knows or has experienced something, transfers that something (resources of wisdom, information, experience, confidence, insight, relationship, status, etc.) to a mentoree, at an appropriate time and manner, so that it facilitates development or empowerment."[4]

There are three big points in this definition that are helpful in comparing mentoring and coaching.

1. The mentor has knowledge or experience the protégé (or mentoree) wants or needs.

2. The mentor transfers that knowledge or experience to protégé.

3. The purpose is the development and empowerment of the protégé.

Scripture is full of these learning relationships: Moses and Joshua, Elijah and Elisha, Eli and Samuel, Ruth and Naomi. By Jesus' time, this model of the mentor-protégé (or master-disciple) relationship had been prevalent for centuries in both Greek and Hebrew cultures. As we know, Jesus' closest followers were called his "disciples."

When Jesus called his disciples, his request was significant: leave everything and follow him. This was more than sharing coffee a couple times a month. He took the mentor-protégé model to another level, choosing to mentor the Twelve within the context of relational proximity. They lived together.

This is a lot of work! It's no wonder that ministry leaders shy away from the idea of mentoring someone in this way. It's a daunting commitment of time, money, and energy. In this day and age, it can even feel a bit overboard or excessive.

Yet, we tend to think these kinds of learning relationships are the ideal paradigm by which we should develop leaders. Leadership development then becomes an all-or-nothing proposition. And many shy away from it because of the high commitment.

Mentors don't have to take an all-or-nothing approach. The key is that mentors put in. They share their input and guidance for the benefit of the protégé. Difficulties in mentoring relationships arise when:

- The mentor becomes too attached to her own guidance and disempowers the protégé.

- The mentor doesn't have a good answer, but gives one anyway to be helpful.

- The mentor's experience and guidance doesn't align with the protégé's needs.

- The protégé's personality and giftedness requires her to approach the situation differently than the mentor would.

Now, let's take a look at coaching.

Coaches Draw Out

When I lived in Japan in the 1990s, I sought mentors to help me design a strategy to effectively begin new churches. My Japanese partner and I interviewed dozens of experienced people. They each shared their experience and gave us their advice. The trouble was, there was something missing from each person's strategy that restricted his or her results.

The question that puzzled us was, "If no one knows, then how do we learn it?" That's when we discovered coaching.

If mentors "put in," coaches "draw out." The difference is mainly in the amount of advising versus asking, as demonstrated by this diagram.

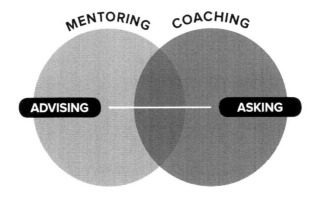

Figure 1: Comparing Mentoring and Coaching

Coaching is a non-directive conversation in which the coach asks a person questions to prompt reflection into what God is saying to that person. The coaching process empowers the person to develop custom solutions for his or her problems or goals.

There are three big points in this definition that are helpful in comparing coaching to mentoring.

1. Coaching is non-directive, that is, the coach does not share his or her experience or guidance.

2. Coaching prompts reflection in the coachee through profound listening and asking powerful questions.

3. Solutions come from the coachee's reflection and creativity, not from the coach.

The use of powerful questions prompts reflection and creativity that produce customized solutions. These results often go well beyond the experience of either the coach or coachee. The process can actually generate new learning.

Coaching works because it brings out a person's best—what God put in. Coaching is based on the biblical understanding that every believer already has an advisor—the Holy Spirit.

Jesus explained the Holy Spirit's role in a believer's life: "But the Counselor, the Holy Spirit, whom the Father will send in my name, he will teach you all things and will remind you of everything I have said to you" (John 14:26).

Christian leaders are not a substitute for the Holy Spirit. Sometimes we forget this and jump into teaching or advice-giving before the other person has had a chance to reflect what God might be saying to them.

Coaching encourages discovery through questions. Advice giving is kept to a minimum so the coachee can discover Holy Spirit-inspired solutions. Advice giving can short-circuit the "discovery" process and put the coach in the driver's seat. What happens is the coachee passively receives the advice and may feel he or she will offend the coach if he or she does not do as the coach advises.

I see my role not as a solution-provider, but as an equipper. A minister's role is to equip others for ministry (Eph. 4:12-13). When I give advice, make the decision, do most of the work, or overly direct I am not equipping others for ministry.

One way I equip people is to help them learn to find solutions by hearing from the Holy Spirit, thinking through options, and making good decisions. Passing on these skills and the authority and confidence to do them are essential to producing an effective ministry.

I believe that by tapping into the Holy Spirit's wisdom, people can create their own best answers. Good coaching will support them in that process. In Proverbs 20:5 we read, "Though good advice lies deep within a person's heart, the wise will draw it out."

However, difficulties in coaching arise when:

- The person coaching has specific knowledge or experience the coachee wants to learn.

- The coachee expects to receive guidance and advice, rather than create her own solutions.

- The person coaching isn't skilled at drawing out and prompting reflection without advising or teaching.

This last reason is why I believe so strongly in quality coaching training. It is too easy for us as ministry leaders to fall back into giving our ideas or constantly teaching. Our solutions can disempower the leaders we are trying to develop by preventing them from creating their own solutions and next steps to act on them.

Quality coaching training does not force us to use coaching at the expense of mentoring. Instead, it allows us to carefully and intentionally use of both types of helping.

In practice, there is a large overlap between these two leadership functions. The reality is, mentors listen and ask questions and coaches provide guidance at times. Sam Metcalf, the President of Church Resource Ministries told me,

"The best mentors I've had have been excellent coaches." The use of coaching skills can make you a better mentor.

Yet, they are distinct approaches to helping people.

When to coach:

- When you don't have good answers, and sometimes even when you do.

- When the coachee needs to learn how to create his or her own solutions.

- When the coachee has a lot of experience in the topic at hand.

When to mentor:

- When you have experience that lines up well with the protégé's needs.

- When the protégé needs doors unlocked for which you hold the keys.

- When the protégé is gifted in adapting ideas and models to implement her own version, rather than simply copying models "as is."

We need both mentoring and coaching. Knowing the difference and being able to do each will expand your leadership effectiveness as you work with people in different ways according to their needs.

How To Bring Coaching Into Your Organization

Coaching requires a shift in your mindset.

It can be challenging to apply coaching mindsets and skills when we hold a position of authority. Despite all the talk of empowerment and being servant leaders, it is all too easy to default to command and control when it comes to leadership. Give someone a title with a bit of authority and they will often shift their leadership style to a command-and-control approach. The old saying, "power corrupts," is mirrored in our everyday attempts to get things done in situations where we have authority. It is just too easy to use our positions of authority to tell people what to do.

A large part of the problem is our misconception that authority comes with the obligation to be directive. Supervisors can always choose to be directive, and in fact, must at times. But a highly directive supervisor can easily find himself or herself micromanaging and disempowering others.

Coaching is often used in conjunction with other leadership roles and tools. We still need to cast vision, assign appropriate objectives, and hold people accountable for their work. A coaching approach can enhance these more directive functions.

The empowering supervisor uses his or her authority when appropriate but regularly cultivates the self-responsibility of others through coaching style interactions.

Ten years ago, many organizations were wary or even suspicious of coaching. That sentiment has changed. Organizations are now, by and large, attracted to coaching. And embracing it. A 2014 UK study showed 76% of organizations offered coaching or mentoring[5]. Coaching has become a preferred learning tool in corporations, nonprofits and churches.

Why the change of heart? A lot of positive results from coaching have been documented. These results, coupled with a global recession where organizations expected more from fewer employees, has catapulted coaching to a preferred method of people development.

Who Gets a Coach?

It's not just the top leaders who get a coach. Coaching is used at all levels in organizations, and my recommendation is for you to do the same in your ministry.

Let's look at the 2015 Executive Coaching Survey done annually by Serpa Coaching out of Dallas, Texas[6]. Sherpa Coaching asked organizations "Who gets a coach?" and sorted answers according to: Top Executives, Senior Managers, and All Levels.

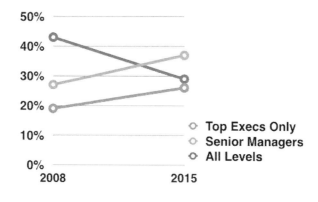

Figure 2: Who Gets A Coach? (Source: Sherpa)

The trend from 2008 to 2015 shows Top Executives and Senior Managers are taking a higher percentage of the coaching, while All Levels has greatly declined. This may seem like organizations are retreating from coaching for those not in Executive or Senior Management positions. But this isn't the case.

Remember this is an Executive Coaching Survey. The coaching people have in mind are largely executive coaches hired from outside the organization. Other people inside organizations are now carrying more of the coaching load.

3 Kinds of Coaches in Organizations

Coaching takes place in organizations at several levels and from different types of coaches. There are three main types of coaches in organizations. A recent study asked organizations about their use of three types of coaches[7]. You might be surprised who is doing most of the coaching.

1. External Coaches. Sometimes called Executive Coaches, these are expert coaches hired from outside your organization. The study showed fifty-three percent of organizations use External Coaches. Top leaders overwhelmingly prefer an external coach.

Advantages of an External Coach include an outside perspective, a safer setting to discuss sensitive issues, and the coach's ability to challenge the senior leader's assumptions. However, they are often expensive. Therefore these coaches are brought in for those who are considered to be higher leverage employees – executives and senior managers. In a ministry context, this might be the senior pastor, or senior staff.

2. Internal Coaches. A growing segment of coaches are those professionally trained and qualified as coaches, and employed by the organization. They function similarly to External coaches, but since they are employed by your organization, they don't require payment to be made to another company. Half of larger organizations employ Internal Coaches.

There are a number of attractive features of Internal Coaches. A big one is the ease and speed by which the organization can deploy them compared to the contracting process of an Executive Coach. Also, as employees of the organization, Internal Coaches understand the organizational culture and have knowledge of internal resources. A few disadvantages include possible difficulty establishing credibility, lack of outside perspective, and demands from other work roles (unless they coach full-time).

Churches and other Christian organizations have identified people with a calling and gifting toward coaching and helped them get the specialized coach training they need to be effective. For example, Send International, a mission organization, has a number of Internal Coaches who are available to coach staff members by telephone around the world.

3. Manager Coaches. These are supervisors who use coaching skills in their regular interactions with those who report to them. Although they may not have specific coaching sessions, they listen actively, ask powerful questions, allow employees to set action steps, and then follow-up.

Organizations are looking to managers and leaders to provide the bulk of coaching for their employees. The study showed 82% of organizations have this expectation of managers and leaders. More and more organizations provide coaching training to equip their managers to coach well. Churches are equipping their small group leaders, staff members, and Sunday School teachers to use coaching skills.

The manager's first-hand experience observing the employee or volunteer in action is a big advantage. Managers are able to have frequent, on-the-job interactions with these folks.

Some of the disadvantages of managers coaching stem from the reporting relationship: too much focus on performance, the lack of broader perspective, and inconsistent types of interactions with employees. However, the potential for healthy change is worth it.

Imagine your entire ministry team utilizing these principles to draw out solutions from one another! Team leaders (particularly those that work with volunteers) will not be seen as domineering personalities bringing their own agenda, but rather leaders who give room for people to grow. Peers within your staff will be able to observe one another in action. The opportunities for on-the-job coaching interactions will be numerous. This could save you hours of personally tending to leadership development and reduce conflict within your ministry, because coaching empowers everyone involved. It is one of the best ways to exponentially increase the impact of your ministry.

Let's move to the next chapter, where we will discover some of the powerful coaching questions you can use right away to draw out insights, strategies, and solutions from those you endeavor to empower.

3.
How To Ask Powerful Questions That Lead To Change

Broadly speaking, there are two ways we learn. The most common way is for someone to tell us something. If we're honest, this is how most of us were raised. Teachers, pastors, athletic coaches and other trainers and bosses have ingrained in us a pathway of informational learning through "telling."

A more powerful way of learning is discovery. Listening to what someone tells you is not discovery. The discovery process requires more effort. You've got to **think critically, dig deeper, and articulate**. The great part is, when you discover it you own it.

Telling can short-circuit the discovery process by settling for someone else's learning instead of pushing forward with our own learning. It is in searching that our readiness to learn and use that learning increases. By thinking hard about a problem we invest ourselves in the process. We own the solutions. And when we discover a way forward, we own that too!

Discovery is powerful because it connects with what we think is important and meaningful.

Discovery is:

Personal. *We are most interested in what helps us.*

Relevant. *We value that which is important to us.*

Inspired. *We hear the Spirit's message to us.*

Motivating. *We want to discover more.*

Infectious. *We want to share what we've discovered.*

Valuable. *We value what we work to find.*

Applicable. *We move when we see ways forward.*

This is precisely why powerful questions are the tools of the trade when it comes to effective leadership development. Yet, most ministry leaders have not been equipped to help people discover. We've been equipped to instruct people. We've learned how to train people. We're experts at casting vision.

Effective and sustainable leadership development is about helping others explore and discover. Here's why.

Adults learn best through dialogue, and questions promote dialogue. Good questions cause people to dig deep in their souls to find answers. Research shows change begins the moment a question is asked[8]. Church consultant Lyle Schaller's experience confirms this. He writes, "The most effective way to influence both individual and institutional behavior is to ask questions"[9].

A Question Is Better Than Your Ideas

Let me speak to why asking a question is better than giving our ideas. This seems self-evident, but when we feel under pressure the "niceties" go out the window. Asking a question rather than giving your ideas isn't just polite, it's smart.

Here are a few reasons why:

- Questions draw out the other person's thinking, ideas, and perspectives.

- Questions increase ownership - the answers are theirs.

- Questions may produce new learning - for them and for you.

- Questions show respect - for their ideas, thinking, and them as people.

Asking questions makes a powerful statement about your trust and respect for the person, and creates greater openness to your input. You can always add something of your own during the discussion.

Questions broaden perspective. Many people are not naturally reflective. Questions are powerful when they provoke reflection in other people, causing them to think more deeply and creatively than they could on their own. There is a trove of untapped creativity and strategy present within all of our leaders. We must get off our well-worn thought paths, and start developing leaders along the road of discovery.

When your leaders start discovering, several powerful benefits manifest for both those individuals and the organizations where they work. Here are three:

- Increased problem-solving skills.

- Increased ownership of insights.

- Increased commitment to action.

Who wouldn't like these results for themselves and those with whom they are work?

If you are like me, you are trying to develop the leadership abilities of others. Discovery is a powerful tool. That's why I like coaching so much. Coaching is a process to help people discover what they need to know, and then how to act upon that knowledge.

Most leaders have not been equipped to help people discover. We've been equipped to instruct people. Discovery-based coaching is about asking questions to help a person explore. This can be done in short conversations that produce powerful results.

If you want to improve your discovery skills, my book *The COACH Model for Christian Leaders*, provides practical ways you can ask powerful questions to help people solve problems, reach goals, and develop their leadership skills, all through discovery.

By helping people discover ways forward instead of telling them, you're building their leadership ability.

How to Ask Questions that Generate Possibilities

Not all questions are equal. Some questions engage the listener, promote creativity, and generate possibilities. Other questions shut down creativity because the question pre-determines a response.

First, let's look at some practical questions you can utilize immediately in your ministry. Imagine a young couple comes to you for advice; they are considering relocating to another city for a new job but aren't sure if it's the right move for them. This couple has booked a 45-minute appointment with you to hear your input. Instead of sharing your well-intentioned advice, imagine what would happen if you asked the couple these questions:

- What parts of this opportunity connect to your calling?

- What might you lose by moving? What do you expect to gain?

- What emotions are you experiencing?

- How might this move affect your relationship?

There's a strong possibility the couple would end up doing most of the talking during the conversation. That also means you can do more of the listening and observing, taking careful note of what they are saying - and what they are not. Perhaps they have overlooked something important. You may catch something they are blind to that could save them years of frustration or regret.

As another example, let's say you are coaching a staff member who is underperforming at his job, and is considering resigning. You might ask:

- How do your responsibilities intersect with your calling?

- What difference would more or less time for your work make?

- How could you organize yourself to see different results?

- How might organizational culture be an influence?

It's not uncommon to have team members that are struggling, or simply lazy. But the roots of those issues are deeper than a mere performance evaluation. Through powerful questions, you can unearth valuable information to diagnose the situation. The truth is, you probably need the answers to these questions just as much as the coachee. Just think of the wider perspective you would obtain of your ministry from this person's answers. If you have a larger organization, think of the insights you and your team would gain from this kind of feedback. It is invaluable.

Questions that Limit

The above examples reflect powerful questions. Contrast those with lesser, limiting types of questions. While seemingly harmless, limiting questions are loaded with subtle hints or implications that can short-circuit the discovery process.

We must refrain from asking questions that have our answers embedded in them. A question that includes an answer ends up limiting the coachee to responding with just a "yes" or "no." This fails to produce reflection in the other person because the options for response are extremely limited. Consider the following limiting questions:

- Are you planning to borrow money to do that? (Guessing the answer)

- Could Susan help you? (Suggesting Susan)

- Do you learn from books or talking with people? (Guessing two answers)

Good questions are like breathing. Physically, we inhale oxygen, which provides energy to our bodies. We exhale toxic carbon dioxide to cleanse our bodies. Questions are to learning what oxygen is to our blood. Questions enrich us, stimulate our learning, and dislodge potentially "toxic" ideas and strategies that we've hung onto too long.

Ask questions.

Though We Have The Holy Spirit, We Still Need The Body Of Christ.

While every believer has the Holy Spirit and thus a direct link to God without a human mediator, growth is not the process of the individual alone. God has set up the Body of Christ as a social setting where God's will is made known, interpreted, and applied. The Apostle Paul wrote that we become mature through the service of the Body of Christ (Eph. 4:12-13). The writer of Hebrews instructs us to keep meeting together to encourage one another (Heb. 10:24-25). The same is true of the leaders you are developing.

When you ask powerful questions, you stimulate reflection in a coachee regarding every area of life, thus leading him or her to the Holy Spirit. In fact, you function similarly to a skilled spiritual director. Richard Foster writes, "What is the purpose of a spiritual director? ...His direction is simply and clearly to lead us to our real director. He is the means of God to open the path to the inward teaching of the Holy Spirit"[10].

I know all this talk of powerful questions and discovery can be scary. As leaders, we're used to being in control. Asking open questions requires that you to give up control of the other person's response. The response to an open question can go in a hundred different directions. But creativity and new possibilities only emerge when we move beyond what we know, and explore what could be.

Coaching works best when both the coach and the coachee trust the Holy Spirit and maintain a listening posture. Spiritual maturity is the ability to hear from the Holy Spirit and put that guidance into practice. Developing leaders within this kind of context results in a healthier, more effective ministry.

Start weaving these questions into everyday conversations, and you will start seeing greater impact with less stress and frustration.

4.
A Better Leadership Development Blueprint

Once you start weaving powerful coaching conversations into the fabric of your daily conversations, you will lead with more confidence and your team will be energized to face upcoming challenges. In turn, your leaders will be able to take these useful, practical questions and utilize them in their respective ministries. The result is a paradigm shift that empowers leaders, values authenticity, refreshes people spiritually, and gets results.

But how do you take the principles of coaching and use them even more intentionally to develop your leaders? Should this entire paradigm shift be systemized? Are there some "best practices" out there, like how long or short a coaching conversation should be, or how often they should take place?

While the answer is a resounding "yes," I also want to remind you to treat this paradigm shift as a process, not a project. It will take time, mistakes will be made, and you will face a temptation to throw in the towel. This chapter was written to give you a few guidelines so you can keep your feet in the running lanes and move past the hurdles.

Let's take a look at several professional studies. Since these studies have numerous data points taken from actual coaching clients, they provide a great starting point for how we can frame out the nuts-and-bolts of coaching within your ministry.

A study by Coaching Research Institute LLP[11] polled coaching clients about the behaviors and structures their professional coaches used and the resulting effects on clients. Significantly, those surveyed were *clients* not coaches, as in most coaching studies. Ninety-three professional coaches from 14 countries did the coaching. The survey measured 22 results clients received from coaching such as:

- I achieved goals set at the start of the coaching engagement.

- I am satisfied with the coaching engagement.

- My direction and vision have become clearer.

It also measured 18 behaviors of the coaches, including the coach "listened until I finished speaking," "I felt safe to share," and the coach "did not impose his/her ideas." Here's what the survey found and how you might be able to increase the effectiveness of your coaching conversations by being intentional with the structure.

1. The Length Of Coaching Conversations

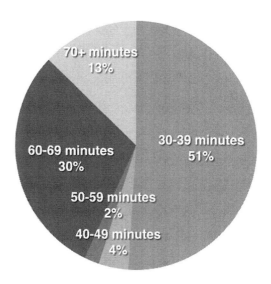

Figure 3: Length of Coaching Sessions (Source: CRI)

How long are your coaching conversations?

You might be surprised to learn that 50% of coaching conversations were between 30-39 minutes. The second most popular length for a coaching session was between 60-69 minutes.

How did shorter conversations stack up against longer ones?

It turns out there's not much benefit to a longer versus a shorter time. A separate UK study [12] found awareness can actually *decrease* with longer coaching conversations.

Rather than coaching by the hour, how about operating from a results perspective and stopping when the coachee gains new insights that enabling her to move forward?

As with many tasks, having a deadline helps us become more focused and productive. Coaching for 30 minutes, instead of an hour, may help you and your coachee to get a clearer outcome for the conversation and sharpen your focus on achieving it.

2. The Frequency of Coaching Conversations

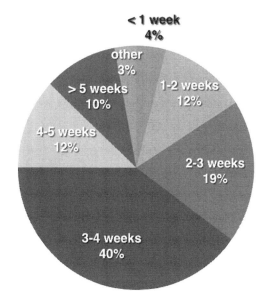

Figure 4: Frequency of Coaching Sessions (Source: CRI)

How often are your coaching conversations?

The study revealed that 40% were coached every 3-4 weeks, followed by 19% every 2-3 weeks.

What coaching frequency correlated with the most positive results?

This time there's a clear winner, and it's 1-2 weeks by far! Nearly every one of the 22 positive effects of coaching was higher when coaching conversations occurred every 1-2 weeks. The majority of the 18 ideal behaviors of the coach were also evaluated higher.

A study of pastors of new churches also demonstrated a link between greater frequency and results[13]. That study found weekly conversations correlated with around 50% greater results than monthly meetings. An interesting side-note is that monthly coaching conversations were actually *less* effective than quarterly ones.

I've long been an advocate of coaching every two weeks. Many people are stuck in a once-a-month mindset, thinking they are too busy to coach more often. But monthly is just not as effective.

More frequent conversations and perhaps shorter conversations may promote better coaching behaviors from you, and produce better results for those you are coaching.

3. The Delivery Method of Coaching Conversations

How do you deliver coaching? The two main delivery methods are in-person and by telephone (or something like Skype). The study showed one-third of coaching engagements were in-person, two-thirds were over the telephone.

Which is more effective, in person or by telephone?

On this point the study focused on the coach's behavior. Clients reported when coaching was conducted by phone, the coach gave less directions and advice from a superior standpoint. The coach also offered more observations on things he or she noticed. During in-person coaching, the coach provided more value-added information through resources such as books and case studies.

Why the change in the coach's ability to remain in "coach mode" over the phone versus in-person? Basically, we have to work harder and concentrate more to coach over the telephone. This heightened state may increase our coaching presence, depth of observations, and keep us so busy listening that we are less tempted to begin teaching or advising.

You and your coachee's preferences do need to be figured in, but overall there is a correlation between structure and your coaching behaviors and coachee results. Shorter, more frequent coaching conversations produce better results.

What This Means For You

The frequency with which you meet with your team members will likely vary according to each person's needs. It is your decision to adjust the schedule as you see fit, but according to these studies you might consider these best practices:

- Keep conversations to around 30 minutes.

- Meet weekly, or every two weeks. Monthly meetings are not as effective.

- Consider operating from a results perspective and finish the conversation when the coachee has gained new insights and a couple of action steps.

- Use the telephone or Skype if you're not working in the same building.

Most ministry leaders make leadership development an event rather than an ongoing practice. We plan for the next big conference, staff retreat, or resource guide to work through with our teams. Eventually, these events either lose their luster or leverage because we don't get the results we want. If we're honest, most of us don't even attend these kinds of events with our expected outcomes in mind. We just attend, hoping for a cure-all, or the next big thing that will completely revolutionize our ministry.

Eventually, event-driven leadership development becomes routine, obligatory, expensive, and inconvenient to our operational schedules. We then cut them out in favor of running our day-to-day operations (we are busy!), simultaneously hardening our cynicism towards training events, resources, and leadership development.

It isn't that conferences, seminars, or retreats are bad. It's that they are feast or famine. To thrive, your ministry needs to "eat" everyday.

Following the findings of these surveys can give new life to leadership development within your organization. Shorter, more frequent coaching conversations may seem insignificant compared to the ministry training conference you attend every year, but they are just as important. I would say they are more important.

Consider how you can set up a schedule for coaching your leadership team. This intentional action and subsequent follow through will result in increased engagement and ownership. You will feel like a light has been switched on and a whole new world has opened up. They will grow in their leadership, thereby increasing your organization's ability to have broad-based impact through all levels. What are you waiting for? Schedule that first coaching conversation.

Coaching Well Requires Skill

Coaching uses some of the counseling, facilitation, and mentoring skills you may already practice. My observation of Christian leaders, however, is that many know *about* active listening and questions, but do not practice them enough in daily life. Christians are partial to "telling" rather than "asking" methodologies: preaching, teaching, lay counseling, mentoring, discipleship, etc.

There is also quite a bit of ego gratification in teaching up front or giving advice to others. It feels like a stronger leadership trait. Coaching, on the other hand, is about drawing out what God has put into the person being coached. It requires a high degree of trust in people and the Holy Spirit to speak to those people. It takes time to learn to coach effectively. It may appear to be much quicker and easier to just tell people what they should do, but that won't develop them to solve problems on their own.

Coaching requires a special set of skills. Below are some of the top coaching skills I have identified:

Listening: taming the tongue

Inquiry: provoking reflection

Feedback: speaking the truth in love

Expanding: facilitating discovery

Focusing: designing actions

Following-up: supporting progress

The time and effort I put into learning coaching skills has paid off a hundred-fold as I coach, supervise, and train others. These skills allow me to more effectively equip and empower others to reach their goals and solve problems.

Coaching Skills Training

Many in ministry call themselves a "coach" or describe their ministry function as "coaching." In Christian circles the term is often used interchangeably with mentoring or one-on-one training. In the business world, the function of coaching has taken on unique characteristics that produce effective results. Producing effective results comes through specialized coach training.

Just as learning to teach or preach required learning new skills and took practice, becoming an effective coach requires specialized training. This training should consist of at least four broad components[14]:

1. Complete specialized training to learn and practice the core coaching skills set;

2. Understand and be able to function within the principles and practices of the coaching relationship;

3. Experience coaching as a coachee, and later be mentored regarding your coaching;

4. Utilize learned skills in coaching others.

A one-day coaching workshop will simply not give potential coaches the instruction or guided practice they need to become effective coaches. Neither will books, internet sites, or audio recordings. Learning to coach requires being with an experienced coach to learn and practice the art and skills of coaching. This can be done in person or over the telephone.

An Increasingly Higher Standard

More and more, the people we minister to are reading and hearing about professional coaching and asking questions like, "Where did you get your coaching training?" or "What qualifies you to coach?" or "Are you certified as a coach?"

That last question brings up the topic of professional coach accreditation. The International Coach Federation (ICF) is the largest coaching association in the world. The ICF set standards for the coaching industry. They created a coaching Code of Ethics and detailed set of eleven Core Competencies professional coaches regularly practice. The ICF has chapters around the world.

The ICF certifies individual coaches and coach training programs. A certification from a coaching association such as the ICF provides an industry stamp of approval, like a earning a CPA or passing the Bar Exam as a lawyer. Beware of coaching schools that "certify" their graduates. Certification is a role of an independent professional association that carefully measures the skills of the coach. A coaching credential is only as good as the rigors it takes to earn it.

Pastors who use coaching skilling skills, even those not wanting to become a professional coach, would benefit from coach training and from engaging in professional coaching standards. For me, joining the ICF and rubbing shoulders with professional coaches encouraged me to move to my coaching skills to a higher level. I think those I minister to are worth the extra effort.

How Christian Coaching Training Helps

Is there anything unique about Christian coaching training? Yes, and there are distinct advantages over marketplace coach training organizations.

Basic coaching principles are very much in keeping with Christian values. Biblical passages illustrate and reinforce coaching values and skills.

For example:

- The Holy Spirit is the real coach, John 14:15-18.

- Listening is an important and difficult skill, James 1:19, 26.

- Be like Jesus, ask questions, Luke 2:46-47.

- The role of a coach is to draw out the coachee's understanding, Prov. 20:5.

- People must think and develop holistically, Mark 12:28-31; Luke 2:52.

Learning coaching skills through a Christian worldview helps individuals and organizations more rapidly adopt a workable coaching paradigm. By matching Christian values, worldview, and beliefs, coaching becomes a way to live out those qualities. Suspicion over whether or not coaching is a New Age practice or just the latest management fad decreases.

By way of illustration, after leading a coaching workshop for Christian ministers, a participant came to me and said, "Wow, I didn't know that coaching was for Christians too. Coaching practices sounded good to me, but until now I wasn't able to make the leap between coaching and my faith." He is not alone.

Unlike some marketplace settings, coaching topics that are Christian or faith issues are welcome in Christian training programs. There is no need to hide or gloss-over the deepest aspects of life. We encourage participants to integrate on all levels: spiritual, character, family, profession, culture, community, etc. The coaching skills and mindsets we teach are completely compatible with and non-offensive to those who are not Christian.

Many people learn paradigms and skills in a secular setting and then have difficulty integrating them with their faith and practice. Given enough time, most Christians can "contextualize" their marketplace training, but by then they have missed the advantages of immediate implementation. The chance of developing new behaviors is greatly reduced.

It's best to take a coaching training that integrates the participant's faith with coaching skills from the beginning. They immediately apply their learning and skills when it is freshest. New habits of behavior are created the day they finish the training. This is a dynamite combination of strengths!

Are You Ready To Coach?

Coaching is a skill as well as a body of knowledge. It takes practice. You can't learn to *do* it from a book. Good coaching training incorporates a lot of time for practice.

My organization, Creative Results Management, has trained thousands of Christian leaders to take their coaching skills to a professional level. I encourage you to join them.

Creative Results Management has developed two coaching skills courses specifically for ministry leaders. The first is *The COACHING Workshop for Christian Leaders*. This 3-day workshop is aimed at learning essential coaching skills. It is useful for integrating coaching skills into your ministry and leadership roles in practical ways.

For those who want to coach more often, the *Coaching Mastery Certificate Program* equips people to the level of a professional coach. The

International Coach Federation approved all of our coaching training programs. With our certificate programs, you can go on to apply for your certified coach credential from the ICF if you wish.

5.
How To Move People To Action With One Simple Question

One of the toughest things in leadership is getting people into action. I discovered one simple, yet profound, question that motivates people to get into action.

People work hard. It feels like we are in action. We have meetings, plan, write proposals, and consult with others. These activities are one type of action. I think of them as planning-action. It's easy to let planning-action keep us from the actions that produce something tangible: launching a program or service and actually meeting people. I call this implement-action.

We need both planning-action and implement-action. This is what James may have had in mind when he wrote, "You see that his faith and his actions were working together, and his faith was made complete by what he did." Implement-action makes our planning-action complete.

It is implement-action when we actually meet people, share the Gospel, launch training for leaders, and make an impact in the world. A lot of us are satisfied with planning-action. It feels productive. However, the ultimate measure of productivity is implement-action.

The Question That Moves People To Action

I discovered a question to help get people into action that is non-threatening and open enough to work in just about any situation. Here's the question:

What actions could you take to move forward?

Simple! But there's power in the wording. Let's take a look the construction of this question.

What... Begin with an open question that will encourage reflection. "Do you have any actions..." is easily answered with one word answers: no, not really, maybe, or yes. Beginning with "what" makes people think and answer in full sentences.

actions... Ask for action but not just one! Ask for actions. Multiple actions will generate deeper thinking and more creative ideas. The results can be combined into one action or perhaps several actions to approach the situation. Think plural.

could you take... "Could you take," will generate ideas a little bit more freely than, "will you take." The "could" removes pressure of having to commit to something upon saying it. I often circle around after hearing their ideas and discussing them, to ask, "So, which of these will you commit to doing?"

... to move forward? This phrase is the key. "Move forward" allows for a process, next steps, and partial completion. It expects progress without demanding everything to be accomplished with this action. If you ask, "What actions will you take to solve this problem?" you are asking for all-or-nothing. It's often too much for one giant leap. People will back off and possibly become defensive. Whereas, "... to move forward" feels quite free, while still understanding that you expect progress.

You can direct the person to a specific area for action by adding the context to the end of the question. So, it becomes:

What actions could you take to move forward on this project?

...with your homework?

...on becoming a better leader?

You can also bridge between planning-action and implement-action by asking:

What actions could you take to move forward in implementation?

...to actually meet new people?

...to start that Bible study?

I encourage you to use this question today with a co-worker, child, or friend. Watch what happens to your conversation and the other person's progress!

Now, I want to ask you: What actions could you take to move forward in developing leaders?

What's Your Next Step?

I firmly believe coaching is the missing leadership development ingredient in many ministries today. I have greater trust in the Holy Spirit's work in people's lives than before. I've felt the burden of having all the answers to people's problems lifted from my shoulders. I've witnessed amazing transformation in the lives of hundreds of people as they have connected to what God called and gifted them to do and become.

These are some of the results *in* me that came from my making a shift in my approach to developing leaders.

How about you? What actions could you take to move forward in developing leaders? It starts with us. As we learn, change, and lead, we become what we want others to become. What changes need to be made in you? Who could help you with that?

Take action today and I believe that you'll be well on your way to multiplying your ministry impact. It won't happen overnight, but you'll be on a path for something great: a healthy, thriving ministry team that is effective at helping people, resolving conflicts, solving real-world problems, and deeply connected to its mission.

Acknowledgements

I dedicated this book to Dr. Steve Ogne, the pioneer in ministry coaching. Back in 1994 Steve published a self-study course on coaching for ministry leaders[15]. A couple of years later Steve traveled to Japan to teach me and other missionaries to ask questions and listen more. I wasn't ready. I had too much I wanted to say! In fact, it wasn't until 2001 that I finally decided to take the plunge and get serious about using coaching skills in ministry. I tell this story in the first chapter of my book, *The COACH Model for Christian Leaders*.

I'm grateful to Steve for always encouraging and supporting me, especially as I dipped into his specialty with my own coaching training. Steve teaches the importance of the character of a coach. The following story demonstrates Steve's godly character.

In January 2007, Steve flew from California to Singapore to attend the second offering of my professional-length coaching training program. Steve said he just wanted to be a participant and learn, but I couldn't stand it and asked him lead a few sessions. Which he agreed to do.

At the end of the week, we sat down at Starbucks overlooking Marina Bay and he pulled out a yellow legal pad with pages of handwritten notes. My heart sank. I thought this was his feedback on what I could do better. He had a few helpful points in that regard, but that's not what his notes were about. Steve had 4 pages of notes detailing what he learned that week and how he was going to implement it in his coaching and training. I was so touched, I cried.

Steve lives out the servanthood that is imbedded in a coaching approach. He puts others first: above his ideas, his desires, and his goals for them. It's Steve's character that both attracted me to coaching and scared me. I wanted to be that kind of leader, but didn't know if I could do it. If you haven't read Steve's book, *TransforMissional Coaching*, don't miss it.

Coaching In Ministry has been cooking for a number of years. I've implemented, taught and written about these concepts with ministry leaders in more countries than I can remember. I knew these things were meant to be in a book, but wanted to get them out right away. It's all well tested in many contexts and with many different types of people. I hope you find it useful.

Many people read over early drafts. I'd like to thank Brad Barshaw, Sharon Denney, Paul Rhoads, Brian Ricci, Dan P., Phil Peterson, Julie Pratt, Bryan Wintersteen, and Kim Zovak for their input.

Mike Kim of http://mikekim.tv stirred, tasted, and added spices to sections so the book would be a cohesive whole. Jason Clement at http://redletterdesign.com plated the meal with his cover design.

I'm grateful to Lori Webb, my wife and ministry partner, for her contributions. She's an excellent coach and trainer of coaches. We began this coaching journey 24 years ago and I couldn't have gotten this far without her. I'm also appreciative to my teenage children, who are my occasional unwitting coaching test subjects. They have taught me to live these principles in day-to-day life.

Most examples in this book are based on actual coaching conversations. Names, locations, and details are changed and are composites of different coaching conversations for purposes of confidentiality. In other words, I'm not talking about you, her, or that guy who told you I once coached him.

Now it's your turn. Are you ready to coach the people around you? They need you.

Endnotes

[1] http://www.intothyword.org/apps/articles/?articleid=36562

[2] S. Kang, "Missionary Attrition Issues: Supervision Perspective of the New Sending Countries." Pages 251-264. In W. D. Taylor (ed.), *Too Valuable to Lose: Exploring the Causes and Cures of Missionary Attrition*. (Pasadena, Calif.: William Carey Library, 1997), 251.

[3] Keith E. Webb, *The COACH Model for Christian Leaders*. (Bellevue, WA: Active Results LLC, 2012), 28.

[4] Paul D. Stanley & J. Robert Clinton. *Connecting: The Mentoring Relationships You Need To Succeed In Life*. (Colorado Springs, CO: NavPress, 1992), 40.

[5] http://www.cipd.co.uk/hr-resources/survey-reports/learning-development-2014.aspx

6 http://www.sherpacoaching.com/
pdf%20files/2015_Executive_Coaching_Survey_
Public-Report.pdf

7 International Coach Federation & Human Capital Institute, *Building A Coaching Culture* (Human Capital Institute, 2014), 8.

8 David Cooperrider, Diana Whiney, & Jacqueline Stavros, *Appreciative inquiry handbook: The first in a series of AI workbooks for leaders of change* (Bedford heights, OH: Lakeshore Communications, 2003), 8.

9 Lyle E. Schaller, *The interventionist: A conceptual framework and questions for parish consultants, intentional interim ministers, church champions, pastors considering a new call, denominational executives, the recently arrived pastor, counselors, and other intentional interventionists in congregational life* (Nashville, TN: Abingdon Press, 1997), 15.

10 Richard Foster, *Celebration of Disciplines: The Path to Spiritual Growth* (New York: HarperCollins, 1988), 185.

11 Coaching Research Institute:
http://crillp.com/en/reports/report01/

12 Carol Gegner, *Summary of Executive Coaching Research Project* (The Coaching & Mentoring Network, 1997)
http://www.coachingnetwork.org.uk/information-portal/Articles/ViewArticle.asp?artId=61

[13] Edward Stetzer, *An Analysis of the Church Planting Process and Other Selected Factors on the Attendance of SBC Church Plants* (A MAMB self study, 2003), 5.

[14] Margaret Krigbaum in Patrick Williams & Sharon Anderson (eds) *Law and Ethics In Coaching: How To Solve and Avoid Difficult Problems In Your Practice* (Hoboken, NJ: John Wiley & Sons, 2006), 67.

[15] Steven L. Ogne & Thomas P. Nebel, *Empowering Leaders Through Coaching* (Churchsmart Resources, 1994).

Recommended Books on Coaching

Collins, Gary R. (2009). *Christian Coaching: Helping others turn potential into reality* (2nd ed.). Colorado Spring, CO: Navpress.

Creswell, Jane. (2006). *Christ-centered coaching: 7 benefits for ministry leaders*. Danvers MA: Lake Hickory Resources.

McLean, Pamela. (2012). *The Completely Revised Handbook of Coaching: a developmental approach* (2nd ed.) San Francisco, CA: Jossey-Bass.

Miller, Linda J., & Hall, Chad W. (2007) *Coaching for Christian Leaders*. St. Louis, MI: Chalice Press.

Ogne, Steve, & Tim Roehl. (2008). *TransforMissional Coaching: Empowering missional leaders in a changing ministry world*. B & H Books.

Starr, Julie. (2011). *The Coaching Manual: The definitive guide to the process, principles and skills of personal coaching* (3rd ed.). London: Prentice Hall Business.

Stoltzfus, Tony. (2005). *Leadership Coaching: The Disciplines, Skills, and Heart of a Coach.* Privately published.

Webb, Keith E. (2012). *The COACH Model for Christian Leaders: Powerful Leadership Skills to Solve Problems, Reach Goals, and Develop Others.* Bellevue, WA: Active Results LLC.

Whitmore, J. (2009). *Coaching for performance: Growing people, performance and purpose* (4th ed.). London: Nicholas Berkley.

About The Author

Keith E. Webb, DMin, is a Professional Certified Coach, author, speaker, and consultant specializing in leadership development. He is the founder of Creative Results Management, a global training organization focused on equipping ministry leaders. For 20 years, Keith lived in Japan, Indonesia, and Singapore where he designed and delivered leadership development programs to Christian leaders in over 30 countries. He is the author of *The COACH Model for Christian Leaders*, *Overcoming Spiritual Barriers in Japan* and is co-author of *Coaching In Asia*. Keith lives near Seattle and blogs at www.keithwebb.com.

COACH Model® Training

Integrate Coaching Skills Into Your Leadership

Are you ready to take the next step and get hands-on coaching training? We teach and practice with you everything you need to coach effectively.

Learn the skills you need to multiply your ministry impact!

Get On The Pro Track

Creative Results Management offers courses in person, online, or by telephone to build your coaching skills.

All of our coaching training has been examined and approved by the International Coach Federation (ICF), the world's largest marketplace coaching association. In fact, you can go on to earn a professional coach credential.

Multiply Your Ministry Impact

Since 2005, Creative Results Management has equipped thousands of ministry leaders in practical ministry skills. We are one of the largest Christian training organizations focused on coaching. Visit our website today.

The COACH Model®

Do you have the leadership skills you need to solve problems, reach goals, and develop others?

The COACH Model® is a radically different approach to leading people. Rather than provide answers, leaders ask questions to draw out what God has already put into others. Learn how to create powerful conversations.

You'll find powerful tools and techniques you need to increase your leadership effectiveness. In this book, you will learn how to:

- Solve problems without having all the answers
- Help others take responsibility for themselves
- Ask powerful questions that stimulate creative thinking
- Create laser focus on what's most important
- Support others to take forward-moving action

The COACH Model for Christian Leaders is packed with stories and illustrations that bring the principles and practice to life. Based on first-hand experience and taught around the world, this book will transform your conversations into powerful learning and results.

Order from store.keithwebb.com

Made in the USA
Middletown, DE
30 May 2015